Friend Grief and 9/11:

THE FORGOTTEN MOURNERS

VICTORIA NOE

Copyright © 2013 by Victoria Noe

Cover design: Rebecca Swift
Editor: Melissa Wuske

Cover photo by Victoria Noe: Empty chairs exhibit at Bryant Park, 9/11/11

All rights reserved. This book or any portion thereof may not be reproduced or used in any manner whatsoever without the express written permission of the publisher except for the use of brief quotations in a book review.

This book is not intended as a substitute for therapeutic or medical advice. The reader should regularly consult a medical professional in matters relating to his/her health and particularly with respect to any symptoms that may require diagnosis or medical attention.

For a list of grief support resources: FriendGrief.com

Printed in the United States of America
First Printing, 2013

ISBN   978-0-9884632-6-4 (paperback)
        978-0-9884632-7-1 (epub)
        978-0-9884632-8-8 (mobi)

King Company—Chicago, IL 60618

Excerpt from *The Guys,* reprinted with permission of Anne Nelson

Excerpt from *Therapy After Terror: 9/11, Psychotherapy and Mental Health,* reprinted with the permission of Cambridge University Press

Excerpt from *Living with Grief, Coping with Public Tragedy,* reprinted with permission of Hospice Foundation of America

Excerpt originally appeared in: Sheridan, Kerry. *Bagpipe Brothers: The FDNY's True Story of Tragedy.* Copyright © 2004 by Kerry Sheridan. Reprinted by permission of Rutgers University Press.

BOOKS IN THE FRIEND GRIEF SERIES:

Friend Grief and Anger: When Your Friend Dies and No One Gives A Damn

Friend Grief and AIDS: Thirty Years of Burying Our Friends

Friend Grief and 9/11: The Forgotten Mourners

Friend Grief and Community: Band of Friends

Table of Contents

Dedication vii
Where Were You That Day? 1
A Hierarchy of Grief 5
Coworkers 15
First Responders 19
Layers of Friends 25
The View from Afar 29
Grieving in Public 31
Celebrity or Coward? 35
A Hole Where a Friend Used to Be 41
"I'm Brian and I'm a Survivor" 45
Surviving, But at a Price 51
"Slán Leat a Chara" 55
Acknowledgements 65
References 67
Resources 69

Dedication

This book is about people who lost friends on September 11, 2001. I have purposely limited it to the attacks in New York City (with one exception). That's because the experience of those who were there and survived was different. There were no survivors in Shanksville. Those who worked at the Pentagon returned to their workplace.

Those who worked in the World Trade Center could not go back, and although not everyone in this book was in the towers that day, the physical landscape has changed forever. Where the towers once stood, there are now a memorial, a museum and new office buildings. That change affects those who grieve the loss of life there that day.

Much has been written about the families, with good reason. Their loss—sometimes more than one person in a family—is immeasurable. In no way does this book diminish that loss.

But I believe it's time—way past time—to acknowledge people whose grief has been ignored or dismissed, sometimes officially.

They are the people who lost friends that day: one, five, twenty, one hundred.

They are the first responders and office workers, the lucky ones who made it out alive.

They are the neighbors and shop owners who watched the towers burn and crumble.

They are the friends who could only watch helplessly as the horror unfolded on TV, hundreds or thousands of miles away.

This book is for them, and for you.

Where Were You That Day?

Everyone has a story about September 11, 2001.

I dropped off my daughter that morning at the Academy of the Sacred Heart in Chicago, where she was in second grade. I didn't have the radio on; she was seven and I didn't like to subject her to news reports. So it wasn't until she got out of the car and I headed to my acupuncturist, that I turned to my oldies station. Instead of music, they were reporting that two commercial jets had deliberately flown into the World Trade Center towers. Everyone was quiet in the acupuncturist's office, and by the time I got back in the car, the Pentagon had been hit and both towers had fallen.

I sat in the car, shaken, not sure what to do. There was already speculation that Chicago was a target, in particular, the Sears Tower. I called school and was assured that all the students were fine; in fact they had all gathered for

Mass. Parents were advised not to pick up their children, so as to not to disrupt their routine.

My husband called and told me to go home and stay off Devon Avenue. Devon is like a little United Nations. The neighborhood changes as you go west: Indian, Pakistani, Jewish. There were already indications that those who attacked us were from the Middle East so it was hard to tell if that was a safe part of town.

Later that day, I would find out that two parents from my daughter's school were in New York that day for meetings at the World Trade Center. One overslept; the other couldn't find his meeting and left before the first plane hit. His wife didn't hear from him until the afternoon. Those kinds of stories were some of the few with happy endings.

We did not allow our daughter to watch the saturation coverage on TV. In fact, she remembers me turning off the television every time she walked in the room. But I was glued to the news. I couldn't wrap my head around it, couldn't understand the scale of destruction and loss of life. I had to try to make sense of something that made no sense.

Several of my classmates from high school and an old boyfriend lived in New York. I didn't call him; though we'd been out of touch for years, I knew enough about his life to believe that an actor had little reason to be near the World Trade Center. The girls, though, I was less certain about. All were in business or law, so they might've had reason to be in the vicinity of the towers. Phone service was spotty, and it took a couple days to reach them.

One, a real estate agent, was now reluctant to go back to work in a high rise. Another, a lawyer, was supposed to be near the towers that day, but wasn't. Still another was at a meeting on Staten Island and got stuck there. There was one more, but I forgot about her until later.

That Friday, as I waited for my husband in front of Holy Name Cathedral before an interfaith service, I called home for messages. There was only one, but I had to listen to it more than once. The woman calling was crying: it was the lawyer I'd known since high school. I didn't recognize her voice because I'd never heard her cry. "Carol's missing," I finally understood her to say. "Her husband's been to all the hospitals but they can't find her. Call school and let them know."

My calls to New York had been out of concern and to ease my mind. I didn't expect to find that they weren't all alive and well. I had no real expectation of bad news. But now, three days after the attacks, we already knew that "missing" was a permanent condition.

I couldn't remember the phone number for our high school, though I could remember it any other time before or since, so I called another classmate and asked her to notify them. By the time my husband joined me, I was crying.

Carol was a Senior Vice President, Corporate Counsel and Secretary of Fiduciary Trust Company International, on the 86th floor of the South Tower. She not a close friend; not a friend at all, really. Her locker wasn't close to mine. We didn't travel in the same circles. Other than going to school together for four years, we had no real connection. But it didn't matter, because the thought of knowing someone who died that day made the horror of the attacks personal.

My husband and I sat in the cathedral, listening to the religious leaders of Chicago recite their prayers and the choirs fill the air with haunting music. Like many people, we went for solace, but that was not something I was able to find, even in the midst of such beauty. The shock of the attacks was just starting to sink in, and the news about Carol made the grief worse. The thoughts going through my head, though, were quite odd.

Carol and I graduated from Nerinx Hall, an all-girls Catholic high school run by the Sisters of Loretto in Webster Groves, Missouri. I sat there, weepy, remembering Carol's naturally curly hair and throaty laugh. But stranger than that, I kept thinking about the Hairy Legs Contest: how long could you go without shaving your legs? If you weren't dating, quite a while. That was what passed for fun in the late 60's. These thoughts were beyond bizarre: they felt sacrilegious. I told no one.

A month or so later, I was in St. Louis for a gathering of about two dozen classmates. We were to discuss a class donation to the school in Carol's memory. At our reunion a year earlier, we'd promised to keep in touch, though no one assumed we would. Everyone says that at reunions. But there we were, together, albeit for a reason no one could've foreseen.

The sangria flowed and eventually I admitted my odd thoughts in the cathedral. One of the women turned to me. "Don't you remember? Carol won the contest."

A Hierarchy of Grief

I stepped out of the subway at Rector Street, about 6:30 on the morning of September 11, 2010. I was in New York to attend observances on the 9th anniversary of the 9/11 attacks. I'd only been to Ground Zero once before, in the summer of 2005, when it was still just a hole in the ground surrounded by security fencing. But this time I had an ulterior motive: I wanted to see what kind of standing a friend could expect. The Memorial was not yet open. Could I attend the Names Ceremony? Would I be welcomed? Would I even be acknowledged?

It was dreary, and the wind was sharp enough to require a sweater or coat. I stopped at Starbucks at Washington and Carlisle for oatmeal and green tea. "The Search Is Over" by Survivor played in the background, and I wondered if I was the only person who thought that was an odd selection. I sat in the window, watching

NYPD and other officials in their dress uniforms or riot gear patrolling the area. Some were putting up barricades, others directing traffic. They always checked for identification and letters verifying that that person was a family member of someone who died that day. The letter was their pass for entrance to the Names Ceremony.

Once I finished my breakfast, I wandered around. I already knew that spectators were relegated to the east side of Broadway, across from Zuccotti Park; the park was off limits to all but participants. But I'd already decided to get a sense of what was possible for someone who had only lost a friend nine years earlier.

"Friend, not family," I'd announce as I approached various police officers in the area. Each would smile apologetically, shake their head and suggest "Just go until someone stops you." I wandered around in circles, always met with polite firmness. The Burger King at Liberty and Church on the west side of the park was as close as I could get without being a relative, dignitary or a member of the press.

I asked several police officers if there was a way to find out if anyone was there from Carol's family. Surely they would allow someone to represent her. But no one knew of any central list keeper who could give me that information.

After a while I gave up and found a spot behind the barricades on Broadway. Before the ceremony began, I struck up a conversation with a young man who said it was his first time at an observance, because it was a Saturday and he didn't have to work. He seemed surprised that it had been nine years: surprised so much time had passed since he watched the towers fall on TV. Thanks to the huge speakers in Zuccotti Park, we could hear the names read, but could see nothing happening across the street.

Although the Names Ceremony had been held every year, this was the first observance, by all accounts, that had political undertones. Tensions were high because of the Park 51 project: a Muslim community center expansion two blocks away from Ground Zero. Although it had been in existence for a while, many objected, believing it violated the concept of "hallowed ground". One protestor carried a sign that read "Mohammed was the first terrorist: Bin Laden's following directions". There were other signs, but none of them are repeatable here. At least they were several blocks away. That morning, though, the people dressed as New York Lottery balls—one ball wearing a police officer's hat, the other dressed as a firefighter—seemed much more disrespectful as they posed for pictures with tourists on Broadway across from the ceremony.

Vice President Biden was attending, so security was tight for that reason, too. I noticed several men on the roof of the Burger King. At first I thought they were construction workers, calling dibs on a great view. Then I realized they were dressed in black, with no hard hats, and they weren't taking pictures. When a shift apparently changed, and the men picked up dark, rectangular shaped "luggage", I realized they were snipers. Flags all around were lowered to half-staff. The windows of surrounding buildings were surprisingly empty: no one was watching from their offices.

All around the area, the police presence was plainly visible. Bomb squad members roamed up and down the street. I made sure to avoid eye contact with them, because I couldn't help but think of the joke I saw in the NYPD museum the day before, attributed to an emergency services officer who died on 9/11: "Never play catch with a bomb-sniffing dog. You never know what he'll bring back."

I marveled at the sheer number of uniformed contingents from around the country who were attending the ceremony: police, fire fighters, emergency response teams, ROTC units, American Airlines flight crews. There were protestors, though not closer than two or three blocks, and they were silent while the ceremonies were taking place. As it turned out later on, the loudest bullhorn belonged not to those who opposed the Park 51 project, but to a minister who ranted against abortion. Anyone with a cause took advantage of the crowds and media attention.

I made a note that morning about how the hierarchy of grief looked to me:

> family > friend
>
> firefighter > police officer
>
> resident > survivor

Families were at the top, and as I said before, deservedly so. Anyone who was not a family member was excluded from the official observances and other events.

Firefighters, based on the sheer numbers of those lost, were held in higher regard than NYPD or Port Authority police officers.

Survivors—those who escaped the buildings—were an afterthought, even more so than displaced residents of the neighborhood.

The strange thing is, even within those categories there are hierarchies. At the FDNY Museum's 9/11 display, there is an explanation of their WTC ribbon/medal campaign to recognize their members. All medals included "343": the number of active duty firefighters who died that day. Any FDNY member who helped with the recovery efforts at any time could wear that pin. Those who were on the site within 24 hours and stayed until the end of the recovery had a star on their medal. Actual survivors were designated with two stars.

I thought about this a lot as I stood in front of the case. Were these distinctions an effort to honor those who sacrificed time, energy and health to search for the remains of their fellow firefighters? Did people's eyes fix on that medal and ribbon, only to make assumptions about the measure of the man wearing it? Did those who had two stars on their pin deserve more respect? Did firefighters judge each other?

A year later, I was back in New York for the tenth anniversary and the opening of the Memorial. I wanted to see what, if anything, had changed.

I wish I had a dollar for every time I heard someone say "Everything's different this year." It was true, for reasons both good and bad.

If tension was high the year before, it was off the chart in 2011. It was a *big* anniversary (you know, one with a zero in it) and the Memorial was opening (but only to family on the 11th). There had been credible threats, as they say, and the city was on edge. I stayed out of the subway, for the most part, though there were enough police in the stations and on the trains that my feelings evolved from unsettled to accepting to defiant: *What are they gonna do? Bomb the R train at 6:30 on Sunday morning?*

More than previous years, there were dozens of events and exhibits held around the city, all very different. There were dance recitals, films, plays and readings. Religious groups held vigils. Academics gave lectures. I planned my week carefully; no more than four events a day. It was exhausting but fascinating.

Once again, I spent September 10 near the site, visiting Trinity Church and St. Paul's Chapel. Trinity Church, near Ground Zero, hosted a twenty-four hour marathon of live musical concerts in their sanctuary. At St. Paul's Chapel, damaged when the towers fell, the usual permanent exhibits were enhanced by a sea of white ribbons tied to the wrought iron fence surrounding the chapel and its historic graveyard: ribbons that had been inscribed by passersby with prayers and the names of those who died. Farther uptown, Bryant Park's great lawn, usually open and full of picnickers and tourists, was filled with row after row of empty green folding chairs, one for each person who died on 9/11, all facing in the direction of the towers.

I attended a benefit performance of *The Guys*, a two-person play by Anne Nelson that was written not long after the attacks. Based on a true story, the play introduces the audience to an FDNY captain who lost eight men when the towers fell. He's been tasked with giving their eulogies and is referred to an editor for help with writer's block.

I'd say the crowds on September 10 were equal to the crowds on 9/11 the year before. Tour groups met near the subway stations, and vendors hawked commemorative photos. The Burger King and souvenir shop were busy. People lined up around the block to leave flowers and take photos of Engine 10's bronze relief memorial on the side of their station. Though generally respectful, the crowds had a bit of a touristy feel. I was interviewed by a journalist from Argentina who was nervous about what she perceived to be a lack of police presence. Her only questions were "Why are you here?" and "Do you feel safe?" I assured her that I did.

Despite the heightened security—you could be asked to produce a photo ID at any time—the morning of September 11 I was able to get closer to the "action". I stood at the northeast corner of Liberty and Church, where a Burger King sits across from Zuccotti Park and the 9/11 Memorial as well as the construction of the Freedom Tower and additional office buildings. The weather was perfect: another clear blue sky reminiscent of the day ten years earlier. The intersection was crowded, but not jammed, and a diverse, respectful crowd stood facing a contingent of Canadian and British police officers, whose perfect formation for over three hours was impressive to behold: dozens of them, line after line, were as silent as the guards at Buckingham Palace, moving only to present the colors whenever there was a moment of silence.

The police had handed down strict rules for anyone in our area: searches of purses and backpacks, photo ID's, no signage, etc. They were not just enforcing safety measures, but ensuring respect for the event. Most people complied without argument. There had been enough tension in the city all week that these restrictions had become sadly common.

Nevertheless a woman right behind me loudly complained for some time to anyone who would listen. She'd been prevented by police from unfurling a huge banner and setting up tables so she could hand out information about her wounded warrior organization. There were places for that, farther away, but she was demanding space on Church Street. I ignored her as best I could until she began insisting to those around her that President Obama had "no right" to be there. That's when I couldn't stop myself. I turned around and demanded she repeat herself, which she gladly did. I told her it didn't matter how she felt about him, he was the president and he had every right to be there. The day was supposed to be about honoring those who died, not making political statements. She didn't say another word and no one else complained about anything.

A Jumbotron was erected on the northwest corner of the intersection so that spectators could watch the musicians, politicians and families during the ceremony. As soon as the ceremony began, everyone in the crowd stopped talking. Between readings of the names, Paul Simon and James Taylor sang; Yo Yo Ma performed. Presidents Obama and Bush, along with Governors Christie and Cuomo read beautiful passages. Something about the voices, interspersed with music, was amazingly soothing. A bell rang six times, followed by a minute of silence, at the exact moments each tower was struck and fell, as well as the attack on the Pentagon and airplane crash in Pennsylvania. You could hear a pin drop.

The year before, the names of all those who died—in New York, Pennsylvania and the Pentagon—were read by family members and construction workers who were building the new tower. I was irritated by that—why weren't friends and survivors allowed to read? Why include strangers who are working on the new buildings?

But mostly I was irritated that my classmate's name was mispronounced. I watched the reading of names on TV in previous years, and the readers never got it right. After years of cringing, I decided that was no longer acceptable.

I spent several months—with the help of Voices of September 11th and Mayor Bloomberg's office—telling the correct pronunciation to anyone who would listen. Still, there were no guarantees that whoever read her name would get it right.

On the 10th anniversary I listened closely through the beginning of the alphabet, and held my breath when they got to Carol's name. This time, finally, it was right. My first reaction—somewhat inappropriate considering the setting—was to burst out laughing. But it was the kind of laugh that dissolves into a sob. I turned away from the crowd and left.

Part of my surprise that it was corrected was that I had no standing. I was not a family member. Whether or not her family knew—or cared—about the mispronunciation, I don't know. But it was done, and I was relieved.

Another thing I realized that day was that I'd had no more access to the official ceremonies than those who survived the attacks, the thousands who lost friends that day. And that didn't feel right.

Coworkers

Where do you work? In an office or a theater? On an oil rig or in a school? A gym or a fast food restaurant? Do you have a small number of coworkers, or are you one of hundreds, even thousands, who work for your company? Whatever your work environment, consider this, from *Therapy After Terror: 9/11, Psychotherapy and Mental Health:*

> …many patients were "suffering differently" because they have sustained an inconceivable number of losses in the attack. In some cases, the losses were so staggering that they amount to the "total destruction of a relational world." Therapists treated traders who lost dozens of close friends in the towers, police officers who lost everyone in their unit, firefighters who

"knew 100 people who were dead," and former employees of "Windows on the World" who had skipped work the day of the attack, with the result that "everyone they know is dead."

All right, stop: read that paragraph again. Now think about your workplace, not just the people who work next to you, but everyone—from the bosses to the janitor—and imagine that most or all of them are dead: the people who work over in housewares, the ones saving a seat for you in your favorite bar after work, the familiar faces in the break room. The enormity of that loss is hard to grasp.

Brian Branco was a consultant for Thomson Financial/Baseline Financial Services on the 78th floor of the South Tower. When the first plane hit the north tower, there was no immediate plan to evacuate their building. But he and his friend, Steven Weinberg, decided to go downstairs to see what was going on and come back up. As they were leaving, Branco's friend said he forgot something in his office. "I said ok, I'll see you downstairs. Steven died..." Branco recalls.

When he got down to street level, there was great confusion. Security was pushing people into the underground mall, because of all the debris at the exits of both towers. Then the police pushed people out on the street. When the second plane hit, he was a block away. In all, three of the five people he worked with died.

Branco's office reopened in New Jersey, with three additional moves in Manhattan since then. That situation is common. Many World Trade Center businesses initially moved out of the city, adding to the disruption to survivors' lives. If their company survived the attacks—and not all did—they had a new, drastically different commute.

On Top of the World: Cantor Fitzgerald, Howard Lutnick and 9/11—A Story of Loss & Renewal is Dave Barbish's account of the company hardest hit that day, losing 658 of the 960 people who worked in the World Trade Center. One of their former employees admitted she couldn't look at her wedding pictures because the whole wedding party was now dead.

It wasn't just that someone you knew died. A lot of people you knew died: bosses, support staff, colleagues. You worked with them, rode the train into the city with them, socialized with them. And now your place of business is gone, too.

What do you do? Where do you start? And where the hell's your desk?

For Frank Walczak, the solution was to keep busy: do as much as possible for as many hours of the day as possible. He and his wife started helping other Cantor Fitzgerald families in their community, but after a few days, that wasn't enough. When the company re-opened for business on Monday, September 17, Walczak began making the three hour drive to their Connecticut office. He found a desk and a phone, sat down, and started working. It was so chaotic it took three days for someone to ask who he was. But he felt useful, felt he was moving forward in some way: for himself, for the company and for the friends he mourned.

The surviving employees of Cantor Fitzgerald were lucky: they still had a company because they followed Howard Lutnick's lead and rebuilt it. Some people—like those who worked at Windows on the World, but were not scheduled that day—lost their jobs. Their place of employment would never reopen. They had to find a way to replace their income.

Those people—those lucky ones—now had to find work, while coping with the aftermath of surviving hell.

First Responders

In New York for the 10th anniversary of 9/11, despite the tension of perceived threats, I felt safe. In fact, I felt like I was surrounded by first responders: not just local, but from around the world. We've come to expect this after tragedies involving police or firefighters: their comrades from other states and countries show up at the funerals to show their respect. If you wore the uniform, no matter where you work, you're one of them.

Everywhere I walked, particularly downtown, I was surrounded. Police and firefighting contingents from Canada, the UK and Australia in particular seemed to be my constant companions. After I left the Names Ceremony, I walked over to the Queen Elizabeth II Commemorative Garden in Hanover Square Park between Spring and Pearl. Later in the afternoon, there would be a ceremony to remember those from Great Britain, Canada and

Australia who died on 9/11. I sat in a café with a couple dozen men and women who'd come to New York—at their own expense—to pay tribute.

I chatted with a number of them, including a young police officer from Canada. I asked if this was his first time coming for the anniversary. No, he said, it was his seventh. After getting over my initial shock (he didn't look old enough to have been out of high school that long) I said I assumed he knew someone who had died, but he didn't. He'd been criticized back home for making the trip, told "this isn't about us." But it is, he said firmly. It's about all of us.

That's the camaraderie of first responders, the sense of shared duty. It creates the cohesion that enables them to work so well together, and identify with those are also "on the job". They may not have known anyone who died that day, but they felt responsible for showing respect.

There were many first responders in New York who did not rush down to the Twin Towers. They had to remain at their stations. But they, too, were affected. One of the most powerful books on 9/11 is Dennis Smith's *Report from Ground Zero*, which contains first-person accounts from firefighters. For dispatchers, the helplessness was palpable. So was the guilt of sending men to their deaths.

You can debate the wisdom of sending so many into the towers. You can discuss the failure of communication equipment between FDNY and NYPD. But you cannot ignore the numbers of people and relationships that were lost. When you consider these were firefighters who lived and worked together, you begin to understand the devastation on a departmental and personal level.

Twelve ladder companies and three engine companies lost every person who answered the call that day. Of the five rescue companies that responded to the attack on the North Tower, no one survived. Not just rank and file were lost: 46 lieutenants, 21 captains, 23 chiefs, including the chief of department and a chaplain, Father Mychal Judge.

The numbers for the NYPD and Port Authority were smaller, but no less important: 23 New York police officers and 37 Port Authority officers. On a departmental level, the FDNY losses were greater, but on a personal level, they were all equal.

Another survivor is Chicago Police Superintendent Garry McCarthy, who was NYPD Deputy Commissioner for Operations on 9/11. Like many who were there that day, he has a couple of gaps in his memory. He remembers being in the command center of the South Tower with Joe Esposito, discussing whether to stay inside or go out to look for the mayor, who was already on the scene. The next thing he remembers is being in the basement of 150 Barclay, just north of the South Tower, where he and others—including Giuliani—were trapped briefly after that tower fell.

McCarthy has the controlled bearing of a man who grew up in a military family and has devoted his life to public service. He rarely speaks of 9/11. In an interview for the *Chicago Sun-Times*, he admitted to losing thirteen friends that day, two of them among his closest. McCarthy spent time on the pile (the name given to the site during the recovery efforts), and luckily suffers no ill health from that experience.

I was grateful for the opportunity to interview him a few months after the 10th anniversary. I expected a very brief discussion. "I know you don't like to talk about 9/11. We can just talk about how police officers cope with a line of duty death," I suggested. That's where we began, but after just a few minutes, McCarthy opened his middle desk drawer and pulled out a stack of holy cards, bundled together. He began shuffling through them as if they were playing cards, but with far greater respect. As he peeled off each one, he told me their name and how he knew them, where he worked with them.

"There were 23 funerals," he explained. "But I only made it to 22 because two were at the same time. We knew that afternoon how many we lost," he said matter-of-factly, and put the cards back in his desk.

The more McCarthy talked about that day, the more passionate he became. He showed me a photo of his car, crushed when the South Tower fell. He has the license plate, a mangled survivor, along with his situation room notes.

He echoed the sentiments of many in the firefighting community, too: line of duty deaths are traumatic in a different way than civilian deaths. You'd think they'd be easier to handle: first responders face death—or its possibility—every day. But their jobs are devoted to preventing death from happening. They're used to being the "good guys". So when one of them dies and is officially tagged a "victim", it goes against everything they know.

Like many survivors, McCarthy spoke with great respect for those left behind: families and friends. I didn't ask what he'd seen when he was working on the pile; I'd heard enough stories and he didn't volunteer any details.

There was a lot of celebrity involvement in the days and weeks after 9/11. McCarthy was one of many first responders invited to the star-studded "Concert for New York", organized by Paul McCartney and held at Madison Square Garden the following month. Instead, he went home—one of his first times home after the attacks—and watched the concert on TV with his family.

It was common for celebrities to show up at the recovery site. Sometimes they pitched in to help; sometimes they were there for a photo op. Mostly they hoped to help boost morale and to thank those who worked around the clock under terrible conditions. McCarthy said that even the biggest celebrities were humbled by what they saw, and could not say enough good about Deion Sanders, "the most respectful man" he'd ever seen.

Only recently, in the spring of 2013, did he visit the area for the first time. His friend, Joe Esposito, was retiring after 44 years of service and McCarthy was in New York for the occasion. They went down to the memorial together, on Esposito's last day at work. "They did a nice job," was all McCarthy said, though he felt it took much too long to build.

Layers of Friends

We all live in a little world of our own. Every day we come into contact with dozens, maybe hundreds of people: barista, waiter, dry cleaning clerk. We talk on the phone to customers, nod to people we recognize in the elevator, notice neighbors in their regular seats on the train.

You probably wouldn't elevate any of those people to the status of "friend", but you "know" them. As we learned in *Therapy After Terror*, when those people were among the dead, entire "worlds" were lost. After all, according to the United States Department of Labor, on the day of the attacks, 368,000 people worked within a few blocks of the World Trade Center. You didn't have to work in the towers to "know" someone who died.

There were 1,100 retailers in lower Manhattan in 2001, nearly 100 shops and restaurants in the World Trade Center alone. Although there are no numbers to quantify the loss, many of those small businesses could not survive the attacks, the toxic dust, the checkpoints, the exodus of residents. They tried: out of a sense of patriotic duty, out of desperation to keep their livelihood going. But their customers were gone: moved away, unable to get through the barricades, or maybe, just maybe, dead.

To understand the scope a little better, consider Northern Somerset County in New Jersey. It had the distinction of having the most per capita losses on 9/11. Hoboken Mayor David Roberts estimated that 1 of every 750 residents were killed in the World Trade Center attack. And Staten Island, New York, home to 5.5% of the population of New York City, was home to 16% of the victims. Those lost were not just family members: they were golf buddies, neighbors, church members, volunteers.

In Anne Nelson's play, *The Guys*, Joan is an editor who volunteers to help an FDNY captain write eulogies for four of the eight men he led. She'd wanted to join the efforts at the recovery site, but she didn't possess the practical skills needed. When asked to help Nick, she jumps at the chance to feel useful. She describes the layers of grief felt by so many survivors of 9/11:

> "Are you okay?" That was what we all kept asking each other the rest of September. What was the answer? The pebble's dropped in the water. The point of entry is you, yourself. Were you present at Ground Zero and wounded, suffocated, or covered in white ash? No? I guess you're okay.

The first ring about the pebble: "Is your family okay?" Did you lose someone in the towers or on the planes.

The next ripple—friends. "Are your people okay?"

Next ripple: If someone died in the tower that you had dinner with once and thought was a really nice person, are you okay?

Next: If you look at a flyer of a missing person in the subway and you start to lose it, are you okay?

(Pause)

If all the flyers are gone one day. They're—gone. Are you okay?

Is anyone okay?

The View from Afar

Not everyone who lost a friend on 9/11 escaped from the towers. Not everyone who lost a friend on 9/11 was even in New York City.

Some people, like me, didn't realize someone they knew was in the towers. Some people believed their friends were not working that day, and initially breathed a sigh of relief only to find out later that the news was bad.

For those who watched the events unfold on TV, there was an overwhelming sense of helplessness. They knew where their friends worked, or that they were in the towers for a breakfast meeting at Windows on the World. They prayed for a phone call that would calm their fears, and hoped they had not just watched their friend die when the towers collapsed.

Bill Rice, head of Cantor Equities in Los Angeles, remembers when the first plane hit. A few minutes later, he saw one of his coworkers sobbing, "He's such a good kid." Rice realized that he'd hired that man's son several months earlier—for a job in the World Trade Center.

On speaker phones, he and others demanded that their New York colleagues go to the roof or get down to the street. But the roof doors were locked and stairways were impassable. They could only listen helplessly as their desperate friends begged for help. They kept their friends on the line as long as possible, trying to comfort and calm them until help was sure to arrive. But they couldn't even call 911: they were 3,000 miles away.

They could only listen to the coughing, the yelling, and finally, the silence.

Grieving in Public

In those first hours after the attacks in New York City, Washington, DC and Pennsylvania, Americans glued to their televisions and radios did not see much of our leaders in Washington. In the immediate aftermath, it was New York mayor Rudy Giuliani whose voice we heard, trying to explain the unexplainable and assure his city that they were safe.

While most people learned of the deaths of friends and loved ones in private, Mayor Giuliani did not have that luxury. Like many people affected, he had no time to grieve: too many more important issues had to be addressed. But during the course of that day, his focus was interrupted three times.

Once was a conversation with his assistant, whose firefighter husband was probably dead. Another was being told of the deaths of FDNY chaplain Father Mychal Judge and the top two men in the Fire Department, all men he'd worked with for years. He didn't learn the news in private; other people witnessed those conversations.

But it was the third time, in front of TV cameras broadcasting around the world, that was captured in the National Geographic Channel 2010 documentary *Giuliani's 9/11*.

Giuliani was answering questions from reporters when told about a woman on Flight 77 who called her husband, Solicitor General Ted Olsen, to tell him that the hijackers were slitting throats with boxcutters. Watching the documentary, you can tell that the mayor is confused by the story, until the moment he understands that it was about his friends. Giuliani pushes down his reaction and continues with the press conference, until he can finish and allow himself a few minutes in an empty office to cry.

Just as soldiers on the battlefield must remain focused on the task at hand, many people—not just first responders and city leaders—were forced to push down their grief on and after 9/11, save it for some undetermined, far-off "later".

By October, 2002, there were 445 FDNY funerals and memorial services for the 343 men who died that day. Why the discrepancy in numbers? Some had funerals, some memorial services, some both (because families waited to hold funerals until they had remains to bury).

The New York Fire Department's band of pipers and drummers played at all of them, unless (a rarity) the family requested that they did not. For thirteen months, these men—whose own ranks had been affected—paid tribute to their fallen comrades multiple times a day.

Members did their best to maintain a schedule so that they could play for funerals of their closest friends.

Afterwards, after the day's schedule of funerals, they would gather to eat, drink and reminisce. Then they'd get up the next day and do it all again. In *Bagpipe Brothers: The FDNY's True Story of Tragedy*, Kerry Sheridan explains:

> All the band members knew, and took as a part of their duty, that funeral rituals exist more for the living than for the dead. Ceremonial honors serve to convey the importance of a life. Under most circumstances, funerals contribute to healing. But the year following September 11, 2001, taught the band members truths they wished they could unlearn. Like when living for the dead became their life. Or like what happened to firefighter Gary Celentani, who'd ended his own life. Like the skewed celebrity, suddenly having hundreds of "friends" and being the most-photographed men in the Fire Department. For many of the men in the band, getting a perspective on what they'd been through was impossible…
>
> By being present throughout the mourning, the bagpipers had played a crucial role in the nation's healing. Their duty had forced them to cling to the past while others moved forward. They'd talked of how it would never be over, but that autumn, the services did cease, and the pipers were thrown back to a reality in which they were again relatively obscure and their ordeal was an outdated remnant of a terrible

time that most yearned to erase. Over the past thirteen months, death had been a constant companion. They were lonely with company, and alone again without it. But there were other companions. Each other. Old friends would stay, and new ones would come. Each moment of life would be differently cherished than before. The recollections would be shared in the lives they led, though spoken of less and less. In years to come, the pain would ebb, the memory smooth over. But they would never forget.

Celebrity or Coward?

Therapy After Terror described two distinct groups of people killed on 9/11. First were the emergency personnel who rushed into the towers and are rightly considered heroes. Then there were the office workers, trapped in their offices or on the way down. As we saw earlier, their decision to leave (if they lived long enough to make a decision) and their ability to carry out that decision, hinged on many variables.

But the author also describes the lucky ones, the people who survived:

> … in spite of the fact that approximately 15,000 civilians succeeded in escaping the towers by digging their way out of elevators, vaulting over piles of rubble, or sprinting down hundreds of stairs, sometimes carrying those who

were weaker on their backs, they commonly were depicted as helpless victims who passively awaited their rescue from the towers.

Just imagine: you survived the worst terrorist attack in history on American soil. You are forever changed, maybe not physically, but emotionally. And now, the world will judge whether you deserved to survive.

Your story of survival may be dramatic, even miraculous. It may be a tale of selflessness and bravery—or blind luck. It's something you have to come to terms with so you can go on with your life. But it's hard because your experience has made you a celebrity, and that has its dark side.

You didn't have to be a survivor to attain some measure of celebrity after 9/11; you only had to have some kind of a connection. "You knew someone who died that day?" people would ask me, their eyes wide. But instead of expressing condolences, they'd jump in with sometimes bizarre, often insensitive questions:

"How did you find out?"

"Did they find any of her?"

Survivors had it worse, though. Even if they weren't necessarily physically injured, what they experienced attacked every one of their senses:

The smell of burning flesh and jet fuel

The roar of the buildings pancaking

The utter silence, followed by the cacophony of chirping firefighters' PASS (Personal Alert Safety System) devices

The sight of bloody body parts and jumpers hitting the pavement

The sharp pain of toxic dust in their eyes and mouths

It wasn't just strangers who interrogated survivors: it was often their own family and friends. People they turned to for comfort instead asked incredibly insensitive questions. *Did you see anyone die? Did you see the jumpers? Why do you think you made it and they didn't?*

Perhaps the most difficult situation was being approached by the families of those friends they lost, people desperate to learn more about their loved one's final moments: *Did they suffer?* Most survivors were unable to give any kind of solace, but it didn't stop people from asking.

Those who survived the attacks realized quickly they needed to turn to those who also survived: friends and coworkers who understood what they were going through.

Formally and informally, survivors formed support groups. Sometimes they talked only to their own family, sometimes only to other survivors. Others turned to therapy or experienced a deepening of their faith. Some turned inward.

First responders not only had to continue to do their jobs—which now likely included digging through toxic materials for the remains of their colleagues—but had to figure out how to grieve their losses in public.

Many funerals—beginning with that of FDNY chaplain Father Mychal Judge—were televised. Hundreds, sometimes thousands, of people attended. Multiple funerals were held on any given day, but firefighters left behind had to decide which friend's funeral to attend, an unexpectedly painful hierarchy complicating their grief.

Their presence at the funerals—and on the pile—was recorded by media around the world. They were rightly considered heroes, but in private, the reality was very different, as noted in *Living in Grief: Coping with Public Tragedy*:

> In the eyes of the world, the 9/11 first responders performed magnificently. In their own eyes, however, they fell short, haunted by what they wanted to find and could not.

It's hard to imagine the pressure—from others and from within. The public—perhaps even your own family and colleagues—expects you to be stoic, to fulfill their image of a strong hero. You want to spend your waking hours digging at the pile, because that way you can focus on something productive, and you don't believe crying or talking will make a damn bit of difference.

David Halberstam's book, *The Firehouse*, tells the story of his neighborhood firehouse, Engine 40/Ladder 35, at 66th St. & Amsterdam Avenue, near Lincoln Center. Only one of the thirteen firefighters who reported to the World Trade Center returned.

Firefighter Kevin Shea did not survive unscathed: a

serious concussion, fractures to three vertebrae, and a severed thumb, among other injuries. But none were as devastating as the amnesia he suffered. He could remember the ride down to the towers, past burning cars and bodies, a flash of being in the South Tower command center, but not much else until he woke in the hospital days later.

While still physically recovering, Shea began a quest to not just find out what happened when the towers fell, but much more importantly, how he behaved. His greatest fear was that he had run the other way, that he had put his own safety above that of others, and failed his fellow firefighters. Shea's superiors felt that self-doubt was normal for the sole survivor of such a traumatic event, but he needed the assurance of memories. And he knew they would not come quickly or easily, if at all.

He felt others were watching him, judging him. This was not paranoia: it was the despair of not knowing maybe never knowing—what really happened. If he could only know for sure, he could explain.

A few weeks after the attacks, he befriended a reporter, David Grann, who spent the next few months with Shea as he searched for answers. His January 13, 2002 *New York Times Magazine* article created a firestorm, in no small part because of the front cover line (which Grann had protested): "Amnesia at Ground Zero: Was the Firefighter a Hero or a Coward?" To add such a public weight to Shea's personal, unending search feels cruel.

There is no room for the word *coward* in the firefighting culture, so to have it used so sensationally was devastating to Shea and the other men of his house.

If you search online for this article, you won't find that headline, just the one that originally appeared inside the magazine: "Which Way Did He Run?" Decide for yourself if that one is less offensive. To be fair, the reporter never implies that Shea was anything less than honorable, only that the inability to remember details made him doubt himself. But being publicly exposed to such damning innuendo was something no one—much less a firefighter who survived that hell—should have to endure.

A Hole Where a Friend Used to Be

The people who lost friends in the attacks at the World Trade Center have some obstacles to overcome.

There's the whole notion that grieving a friend is not on a par with grieving a family member. If you're like a lot of people, you spend more time at work than with your family, at least during the week. It's not just the work hours: your social life may also revolve around work. When a friend from work dies, there's a hole in your life.

Then there's the hierarchy of grief, where families not undeservedly receive the bulk of attention. But for those who lost friends, it seems there's no room for them. It's not that they seek attention, not in the sense of being in the spotlight. They simply ask for respect for their loss, and respect for their experience, especially if they are also survivors.

Rituals following someone's death serve a purpose:

to honor the dead while comforting the living. Every culture has their own traditions: from sitting *shiva* to military honor guards, from Irish wakes to New Orleans jazz processions. Generally speaking, all are welcome to attend.

From the beginning, the official observances of the September 11 attacks in New York have been limited to dignitaries and family members. My experiences on the 9th and 10th anniversaries are felt even more strongly by survivors. Many of them attend the ceremonies, but can be no more involved than I was: they're shut out. Survivor David Donovan shares his thoughts:

> I fully understand we must honor those who were lost and their families. But we survivors should be included as well. We should be allowed to read names of the victims, be allowed to go to the memorial on September 11th and not have to wait until the next day like the "general" public.

Another survivor, Brian Branco, explains how this policy affects him:

> My family and I have gone to the ceremony every year on 9/11 since it's really the place I need to be. Being a survivor, we have been excluded from everything, as everyone says we are the "lucky ones". The "officials" really need to understand survivors guilt.

Survivor guilt: what many feel, but fewer admit. Another way to imagine this hole is to consider what is commonly referred to as "institutional memory". It's the knowledge of the way things are done. There are people you work with who have been there a long time. They know things that are not written down anywhere. If your company is going to survive, they need to be there or their expertise has to be replaced.

Cantor Fitzgerald was on the brink of collapsing, losing ¾ of their New York employees, many of them the key money-makers of the company. There was never a question of whether to rebuild: CEO Howard Lutnick promised a percentage of the firm's profits to the families, along with healthcare. But how would the company survive?

First they had to reopen quickly, with the staff that remained. Then they had to replace those who were lost, hiring an average of ten new employees every week for months. In essence, they had to create an entirely new company: full of talented people who didn't know how it used to be.

It was the same for first responders. Michael Simon was a rookie firefighter on September 11, when his house, Engine 24/Ladder 5 lost eleven of its firefighters. It's taken the department years to fill the "vacuum of experience" left by the men who passed on their skills to newcomers at the red brick firehouse on Sixth Avenue, says Lt. Michael Thomas of Ladder Co. 5. "They had a wealth of knowledge that they shared with us", says Simon. "Their knowledge, their wisdom made me carry on to this day."

In addition, in the first seven months of 2002, 661 firefighters retired, more than double the number for the same period a year earlier. Their experience, knowledge and expertise compounded the losses suffered on 9/11.

In your job, even in your personal life, there are many things that are just "known." They're not written down anywhere because they're common knowledge. But what happens when all the people who know are gone? What happens when you're the only one left who knows?

"I'm Brian and I'm a Survivor"

When I read Brian Branco's responses to my questionnaire, I imagined him saying these words. I didn't mean it in a flippant way at all, or to suggest that survivors are members of some odd 12-step group. But he opened my eyes to feelings I hadn't considered.

While the word "victim" is charged with emotion and even politics, the designation "survivor" is also one that people who escaped the Twin Towers may be reluctant to adopt. It's a word that denotes some kind of accomplishment, and that's hard to accept:

> It took me a long time to put me and the word survivor together, as a matter of fact, I tell people I worked in the building and I was there that day, but I avoid the word survivor…It took me 5 years to come to terms with that and be able to say, "it just wasn't my time."

Survivor guilt pops up in nearly every story you hear from people like Brian. Some admit to struggling with it more than a decade later. Others worked through it quickly. Not all were able to cope. But it's something they all faced on some level.

Wouldn't you want to survive something as cataclysmic as the September 11 attacks in New York? Of course you would. But as Malachy Corrigan, director of FDNY's counseling services unit, told *New York* magazine on the 10th anniversary, "'Why did I survive?' is still a big question."

USA Today conducted an exhaustive survey a year after the attacks to try to understand who survived and why. Some workers had also been there for the 1993 bombing. Everyone who evacuated after that attack survived, though their trek down to street level lasted as long as four hours. There was no reason to hurry then, so those who lived through that didn't see a need to hurry this time.

Thousands of people escaped from the towers on 9/11, many more than died. Virtually everyone above the point of impact in the North Tower was trapped. The public address system was knocked out by the force of the plane's impact, so there was no opportunity to direct workers to leave.

People in the South Tower had only 16-1/2 minutes (the time gap between the attacks on the North and South Towers) to decide whether to let that first attack guide them. For most of those above the point of impact in the South Tower, the decision to stay put had tragic results. The survey of survivors found that those on the highest floors in the South Tower who witnessed jumpers from the North Tower were most likely to leave their desks immediately.

Keating Crown was one of those people. An associate at AON, he was in a meeting on the 100th floor of the South Tower when the North Tower was attacked. He and his coworkers began to evacuate immediately, a decision that saved many, but not all, lives. Upon reaching the 78th floor, one woman got in the elevator, but Crown took the stairs, just as the second plane hit their tower. She did not survive, but Crown did, making his way down to the street on a broken leg.

Information, too, was confusing: many people in the South Tower remember the announcement from OCS Security that their building was secure. Sometimes the decision to stay or leave was serendipitous: they had a bad feeling; maybe they wanted to go downstairs to have a cigarette or better see what was going on. Some didn't even know what happened until they received calls from friends or family watching on TV.

Area hospitals optimistically prepared for hundreds of patients they assumed would be rescued from the ruins, but only twenty people were brought in, the last one almost exactly 24 hours after the towers fell.

I'll bet that since that day, every one of those survivors heard someone insist: "Hey, you got out. That's all that matters." On a very basic level, yes, that's true. But attitudes like that—common after any kind of tragedy—aren't helpful to those who struggle to answer the question of why. Those who survive an event like 9/11 may struggle a bit more.

Their experience was traumatic, but that was only the beginning. The judgment of the world—family, friends, strangers, media—about their behavior that day only adds to feelings of loss and unresolved guilt.

David Donovan was an investment banker/stockbroker with May Davis Group on the 87th floor of the North Tower. One of his coworkers, Harry Ramos stopped to help a man on the stairs. Both of them died.

> To this day part of me feels guilty for making it out of the towers when so many people I came across did not. I know there was nothing I could have done but I find myself wondering what if I had told Harry to come and not stay behind, what if I would have searched for people on the floors just above us, or grabbed a fireman and said get out. I know it wouldn't have changed anything, but that feeling remains.

There were also survivors who had to escape other buildings. A Chicago mother and daughter, Faye and Leigh Gilmore, were staying at the Marriott World Trade Center Hotel. When the Twin Towers were hit, the hotel was damaged: by jet fuel, debris and falling bodies. The elevators didn't work, and as in the towers, guests were directed to the darkened stairs. For the Gilmores, that was a problem: Leigh's multiple sclerosis confined her to a wheelchair. In the 5th floor hallway, as people rushed for the exits, Faye begged for help with her daughter. No one stopped.

Meanwhile in the lobby, one of the Marriott's engineers, Gregory Frederick, suddenly remembered the woman on 5 with a disability, whose shower grab he and his boss Arnulfo Ponce had fixed the day before. He commandeered the only working freight elevator to the 5th floor and took the two women down to street level. The first tower fell when they reached the street. The women were separated in the confusion, and reunited later in a New Jersey hospital.

For eight years the two women wondered if the men who helped them survived. Every September 11th, the two men wondered if the two women survived. On the 8th anniversary, Ponce's wife was watching a History Channel special, *Hotel Ground Zero*, and saw the two women. Frederick was home watching it, too, and he was stunned.

The men tracked them down online, and a few weeks later, traveled to Chicago so the two women could finally thank them. There were more than a few tears. Less than two months later, Leigh Gilmore died from complications of MS.

Time and again, survivors have told stories of a friend or stranger whose actions saved them that day. A firefighter appeared from nowhere and pushed them into a building to avoid the toxic cloud. Someone carried them when their legs gave out. There in an instant and gone, never to be seen again. Many have called them heroes. Many more have called them angels. Few have learned the fate of the mysterious stranger who helped them. But all wish they could be like the Gilmores, and have one moment to say "thank you".

Surviving, But at a Price

"I'm surprised more of us aren't crazy," admitted FDNY Lt. Adrienne Walsh in *New York* magazine. That sentiment isn't limited to first responders, although in the ten years after the attacks, 11,000 firefighters were treated in the FDNY Medical Monitoring and Treatment Program.

Many factors play into who seeks out and receives counseling after a trauma: culture, personality, profession, gender. First responders, accustomed to being strong and in charge, often resist counseling. After all, they're the people who help, not the ones who need help. They tend to view seeking help as a sign of weakness, one that could potentially impact their employment. These people may open up only to a neutral party—not a therapist or doctor—but someone there just to listen.

Andrea Raynor is a Methodist minister in Rye, NY. She's also an FDNY chaplain, who served at Ground

Zero during the recovery efforts. She blessed body bags of remains, even those suspected to be the hijackers. For eight months she walked the area, looking for people who needed to talk. "Some of the workers were there when the buildings fell and had a lot of guilt because they left people behind," she told *USA Today.*

In *The Guys*, Nick struggles with his grief for his men, and survivor guilt because he switched shifts with his best friend.

He rails against the hero status each has acquired, arguing that they were just doing "the greatest job in the world." He hates that they're being elevated to sainthood when they were just everyday guys. Little by little, he shares the humanity in each so-called hero, the "ordinary" in each man who died doing what he loved.

Dismissing the elevation to "hero" is common among survivors. Even those who were responsible for saving the lives of coworkers or strangers cringe at having their actions called heroic. That doesn't make sense, you might insist. What they did *was* heroic.

But time and time again, survivors—first responders and civilians—refuse the spotlight. "It's not about me," they insist. They don't want the attention. They were just doing their jobs, or doing something that was obviously the right thing to do. They demand that the focus be shifted to their friends, the ones who didn't make it out.

But the spotlight on survivors persists, sometimes at a high price.

Kenny Johannemann was a part-time janitor in the North Tower on 9/11. In one of the many odd stories of that day, his life was spared because he stopped for a cup of coffee, so he was waiting for an elevator when the first plane hit his building. The doors immediately opened and a man fell out of the elevator, on fire. Johannemann dragged him out and to an ambulance.

For his heroics, he received a congratulatory letter from President and Mrs. George W. Bush. Before the seventh anniversary, he was dead: suicide. Depressed since 9/11, he became an alcoholic, cutting himself off from friends and family. About to be evicted from his apartment, he left two letters: the one from the Bushes and his suicide note. He hoped people would remember that he was a good person when he wasn't drinking.

It's impossible to get an accurate count of how many 9/11 survivors have taken their own lives. On the 9th anniversary, the *New York Post* reported that 44 first responders and volunteers had committed suicide. But that number excludes many who were there that day: office workers, residents, visitors. Everyone's lives were so deeply affected that it must be impossible to identify all of those who were in enough despair to end their life.

The Emerald Society Bagpipe Band, the elite group of firefighter/musicians, depicted so beautifully in *Bagpipe Brothers*, was not immune to despair. Playing for multiple funerals and memorial services each day for over a year, they were immersed in the memories of 9/11. Their own grief had to be mostly pushed down, so they could function well enough to honor their fallen comrades. They talked, they drank, they played. And the next day they did it all over again.

I remember being about 2/3 of the way through the book when I realized that one particular man seemed fated to kill himself. I dreaded turning pages, sure that the next would reveal the awful deed. But it didn't happen. He was the obvious choice, the one struggling the most. But he didn't do it.

One of the other guys did.

"Slán Leat a Chara"

Farewell, my friend.

After the 9/11 attacks, many people struggled to find something to do, some way to make a difference, to help.

Firefighters worked on the pile around the clock, digging for remains, because no firefighter is ever left behind. They were joined by police officers and construction workers from around the country. Therapists and other medical professionals volunteered their time to help those most affected. Strangers donated food, supplies, time and money. As Anne Frank said, "Despite everything, I believe that people are really good at heart." That was certainly proven in the weeks and months following 9/11.

Most obviously, people gathered together—in New York, Washington, Pennsylvania, and around the world—to remember those who died.

In 2002, 350 British soldiers attended the first anniversary observances. Although those numbers had dwindled ten years later, the dozens of British, Canadian and Australian officers who stood in formation for hours during the Names Ceremony, and later held their own ceremony in Hanover Square Park, traveled to New York at their own expense. Time and again, they explained their presence was an honor, not an obligation.

The British Garden ceremony and the Buddhist-led interfaith service at Pier 40 were two very different ways of expanding the universe of mourners beyond family members. Although both welcomed everyone, the two much-smaller ceremonies could not have been more different.

The British, to no one's surprise, conducted a formal ceremony in that tiny slip of park near Wall Street after the Ground Zero ceremonies. The officers marched and stood at attention while the West Yorkshire Pipe and Drum Band performed, followed by the Gardens' official bagpipers, The Allied Forces Foundation. A combined choir from Scotland performed, too, after formal speeches by Canadian Prime Minister Stephen Harper and the Consuls General of Australia and Great Britain.

Unlike the morning's commemoration, there were no religious references, no recitation of victims' names. It was proper, sincere and secular.

That night, Pier 40 at the end of Houston Street was turned over for a Buddhist floating lantern ceremony, which I had also attended the year before.

Hundreds of people gathered in early evening to write messages, memories and prayers on large pieces of paper, which were then crafted into lanterns. Each was affixed to a small tray, with a candle in the center. The trays were tied together, in a line of five or six, to form a chain of soft lights. After the sun went down. kayakers pulled them out into the Hudson, where they were released into the night.

There were a few brief speeches, which mainly served to welcome those attending and explain the significance of the music, the lanterns and the chanting. Though referred to as Buddhist, it was quite interreligious, with Jewish, Hindu, Christian, Islamic and Afro-Caribbean ministries included.

Unlike the heavy beat of drums and plaintive drone of the bagpipes in Hanover Square Park, the music here was softly played mostly on delicate reed instruments, punctuated by an occasional gong.

In contrast to the mostly over-40 crowd for the British ceremony, the crowd at Pier 40 was much younger and more culturally diverse. They were mostly New York residents, rather than tourists. It was an incredibly peaceful and restorative way to end the day.

Both of these ceremonies and hundreds more—repeated in communities around the world—gave honor to those who died. But they don't alleviate the hurt many feel, that the official ceremony bars non-family members from participating or formally attending. Survivors, especially, feel shut out.

How then, do people remember their friends who died on that clear, blue Tuesday morning?

David Donovan, who was separated from his friend on their way down to street level, makes donations in Harry's name to various organizations, but he feels his main obligation is to tell people about Harry.

> Harry's selflessness to stay behind with a complete stranger will always stand out for me. He gave his life to comfort a stranger, when he could've just kept walking and saved himself... But the ultimate way I keep Harry's memory alive is by making the most out of every day and helping as many people as I possibly can. I know that may sound cliché, but I know I am truly fortunate to be here and I owe it to Harry and the roughly 3,000 other people to pay their sacrifice forward.

Kristan Exner was a 21 year old law student working as a paralegal on the 52nd floor of the North Tower when it was hit. A military veteran, her training served her well, as she calmly ushered coworkers down the stairs and out onto the street, just minutes before the South Tower fell.

Searching for answers and suffering from the effects of post-traumatic stress, Exner changed her career path in a dramatic way. She not only traded in corporate law for immigration and juvenile issues, but she founded a nonprofit organization, Tails of Courage.

Exner's passion is training rescue dogs as therapy animals for others suffering from PTSD. She herself benefited from the unconditional love of a cat named Otto in the aftermath of the attacks. Like many, she seeks a higher purpose for her life, always with a mind to honoring those who didn't survive.

Brian Branco and his wife volunteer at the World Trade Center Tribute Center, leading walking tours of the area.

The tour gives him an opportunity to talk about his friends, Bob Levine, Jill Maurer-Campbell and Steven Weinberg, because keeping their memory alive is a priority for him. He wants visitors to know that Bob came back to work six weeks after major surgery; that Jill's son crawled for the first time on 9/11, but she never saw it; that Steven was a big family man, and fan of the TV show "Survivor".

Brett Bailey worked for Eurobrokers. In the summer of 2001, he told two buddies, Art Della Salla and Joe Bonavita that they should start having regular get-togethers. They were all young men in their 20's, working in the financial world in New York. So began a series of monthly steak dinners. But on 9/11, Brett, Joe's girlfriend and another friend, Chris Dunne, were killed in the collapse of the towers.

The friends left behind continue to come together—now quarterly, rather than monthly—for a steak dinner at one of New York's best restaurants. After the attacks, they began throwing in an extra $20 each (now each member is simply assessed $240 a year). The money is donated to good causes: Joe's girlfriend's high school or charities founded by their friends' families.

The group has grown over the years, including many who didn't know the three who died. But, for the original members, it was nothing less than necessary for their survival. Their biggest fear—the biggest fear of everyone affected by that day—was that their friends would be forgotten. Over 100 dinners later, they've ensured that that doesn't happen.

Keating Crown decided to honor the families of those lost by serving on the committee that oversaw the design and construction of the 9/11 Memorial, traveling often from Chicago to New York to do so.

Friends of the popular FDNY chaplain, Fr. Mychal Judge, founded a nonprofit organization in his memory, Mychal's Message. They honor his memory in Pennsylvania and New York through their service to children and the homeless.

Superintendent McCarthy believes his experience on 9/11 calmed and focused him to make a difference wherever he is assigned. And it gave him a new appreciation of what his father, a WWII Marine, faced during four years of fighting in some of the biggest battles in the South Pacific.

Michael Lomonaco, executive chef of Windows on the World, stopped to have his glasses fixed before heading up to work, an errand that saved his life. As executive chef of new restaurants since then, he has hired former Windows on the World employees, and aspires to recreate the family atmosphere he and his 73 lost coworkers enjoyed.

For the girls in my high school class, it was the moment when "we should get together more often" actually resulted in action. We don't wait for the next reunion anymore. We meet on an irregular basis for dinner. Smaller gatherings are more frequent. Our Yahoo group is still going strong, now filled with updates on births of grandchildren, moves to new locations, deaths of parents and each other's health. Girls who were not close to me when we sat in Sr. Paul Mary's geometry class are now my friends.

September 11 is now a National Day of Service and Remembrance. People from all over our country choose to spend that day by giving to others, in memory of those who died and no longer can.

But what drives them all, what drives everyone who lost a friend that day, is the desire to keep the memory of their friends alive.

Telling stories—about their friends, how they lived and what their friendship meant—is the common thread among all those who lost a friend on 9/11. They may not want to talk about how they're doing, personally, but they always want to share something about their friend.

He taught me a lot about business.

She loved being a mom.

He sacrificed his life for a complete stranger.

Time passes. People forget. It's human nature, especially the desire to forget something as horrific as that day. But those who lost friends do not have the luxury of forgetting.

For those who lost friends that day, being shut out of the official anniversary services is an insult. That decision says to them "your loss doesn't count." They can't visit the memorial on September 11, because that day is reserved for families. They don't have the honor of reading the names of their friends and coworkers at the Names Ceremony. So they must stand in the crowd blocks away, behind the barricades with the tourists, officially forgotten. They deserve better.

Like them, I had to wait to visit the Memorial, which I did on September 13. I invited that former boyfriend to go with me. Living in Chelsea, he had vivid memories of the day and was anxious to see the Memorial. Mostly I invited him because he was a shoulder to cry on. I hadn't cried about anything in a long time, but I suspected that the Memorial—and seeing Carol's name engraved there—would change that.

Security was still high: no bags or backpacks allowed. Picture IDs were checked several times, and you had to go through a metal detector. Police were everywhere as the crowd snaked its way through the various checkpoints. And then, suddenly, you were there: a quiet, peaceful place near multiple construction projects, next to the West Side Highway. It was amazing just how peaceful it felt.

We went first to the kiosks where you can type in a name and find the location of its inscription. Armed with that information, we walked to the footprint of the South Tower, where I was pleased and pained to find Carol's name. Whether or not remains have been found (and for most victims, none have), whether or not a funeral or memorial service was held, there is a crushing finality in seeing those names.

Unlike the Vietnam Memorial, where the names are listed in chronological order, the names at the World Trade Center memorial are arranged by affiliation, thanks to the efforts of the 9/11 family organizations. The names in closest proximity are coworkers and friends, and I find great comfort in that. After all, in cemeteries, people are generally buried with family members. They're not alone: at Ground Zero, the only resting place for so many, those who died are surrounded by friends.

I did indeed have my cry, though not as hard or as long as I anticipated; hearing Carol's name pronounced correctly turned out to be more emotional. At some point I saw people making rubbings of the names, something I'd noticed on the TV reports from the opening. We found a volunteer, who gave us strips of cottony paper and a thick black wax crayon.

I was doubly glad I'd brought my friend: he's very calm and deliberate, as well as detail-oriented, so the two rubbings we made of Carol's name do not look like a child had done them (which would've been the result if I'd tried to do it myself). On my next trip to St. Louis, I delivered one to our high school.

Later we sat on a bench near the Survivor Tree, a Callery pear that had been planted in the 1970's and was the only tree to survive the attacks. In October, 2001, it was found in the rubble, barely alive. The NYC Park Department moved it to the Arthur Ross Nursery in the Bronx' Van Cortland Park, where it was lovingly brought back to health. Only eight feet tall when found, it had surged to over thirty feet. Keating Crown was there to see its replanting.

You can't miss it: the other 400 trees are swamp white oak, so its shape and color stand out. It's secured with steel cables and protected from enthusiastic visitors who view it as a shrine. Some leave teddy bears or flowers; all take pictures.

When I visited the site in 2005, I felt very anxious, very uncomfortable. But everything about the memorial calmed me: the young trees, the soothing splash of the waterfalls, the amazing lack of intrusive noise.

It's a final resting place, marking a moment in history that changed the world.

And as it turns out, it's a place where people can find comfort remembering their friends.

For more photos of the 9/11 Memorial in New York
and the ceremonies described in this book,
log onto http://pinterest.com/VictoriaNoe/boards/

Acknowledgements

There are many people whose generosity is important to this book.

First, I'm grateful to those people I interviewed, especially Chicago Police Superintendent Garry McCarthy and members of the World Trade Center Survivor's Network. Their willingness to share their stories with me—and with my readers—is deeply appreciated.

My alpha readers (because it sounds better than 'beta'): David Beckwith, Ann Smith and Kathleen Pooler.

I've been impressed with several 9/11-inspired organizations, especially Voices of September 11 and Mychal's Message. They do excellent work and were generous with their time. They deserve your support.

And to my family, thanks for your patience.

References

Baer, Ulrich, ed. *110 Stories*. New York and London: New York University Press, 2002.

Barbash, Tom and OTOTW LLC. *On Top of the World: Cantor Fitzgerald, Howard Lutnick and 9/11—A Story of Loss & Renewal*. New York: Harper Collins, 2003.

DiMarco, Damon and Thomas Kean. *Tower Stories: An Oral History of 9/11, 2ndEdition*. Solana Beach, CA: Santa Monica Press, 2007.

Giuliani, Rudolph W. with Ken Kurson. *Leadership*. New York: Hyperion, 2002.

Halberstam, David. *The Firehouse*. New York: Hyperion, 2002.

Lattanzi-Licht, Marcia and Doka, Kenneth J., eds. *Living with Grief: Coping With Public Tragedy*. Washington, DC: Hospice Foundation of America, 2003.

Lutnick, Edie. *An Unbroken Bond*. New York: Emergence Press, 2011.

Seeley, Karen M. *Therapy After Terror: 9/11, Psychotherapy and Mental Health*. New York: Cambridge University Press, 2008

Sheridan, Kerry. *Bagpipe Brothers: The FDNY's True Story of Tragedy, Mourning and Recovery*. New Brunswick, NJ: Rutgers University Press, 2004.

Smith, Dennis. *Report from Ground Zero: The Story of the Rescue Efforts at the World Trade Center*. New York: Penguin Group (USA), 2002.

Smith, Dennis with Deidre Smith. *A Decade of Hope: Stories of Grief and Endurance from 9/11 Families and Friends*. New York: Penguin Group (USA), 2011.

"Ten Years Later: 9/11 We Remember" *New York Post*, September 11, 2011

"9/11: One Day, Ten Years" *New York Magazine*, Sept. 5-12, 2011 edition

"9/11: A Decade Later", *Chicago Tribune*, Sept. 4, 2011

"Delay Meant Death on 9/11", *USA Today*, Sept. 2, 2002

"NY Firefighter Thinks of 9/11 Dead 'Every Day'", *The Seattle Times*, Sept. 8, 2011

"Chicago's New Top Cop was NYPD's Operations Chief on 9/11", *Chicago Sun-Times*, June 4, 2011

"The Paralegal: 'It was hard to see through the glass. Everything was orange from burning debris.'" *Stamford Advocate*, Sept. 9, 2011

Resources

National Day of Service and Remembrance—
www.serve.gov/

Mychal's Message—
www.mychalsmessage.org

World Trade Center Survivors Network—
www.survivorsnet.org

9/11 Memorial and Museum—
www.911memorial.org

World Trade Center Tribute Visitors Center—
www.tributewtc.org

StoryCorps 9/11 Project—
www.storycorps.org/initiatives/september-11th/

Tails of Courage—
www.tailsofcourage.org

Victoria Noe has been a writer most of her life, but didn't admit it until 2009. After earning a Masters from the Victoria Noe has been a writer most of her life, but didn't admit it until 2009. After earning a masters in Speech and Dramatic Art from the University of Iowa, she moved to Chicago, where she worked professionally as a stage manager, director and administrator in addition to being a founding board member of the League of Chicago Theatres. She then transferred her skills to being a professional fundraiser, raising money for arts, educational and AIDS service organizations, and later an award-winning sales consultant of children's books. Noe also trained hundreds of people around the country in marketing, event planning and grant writing. But after a concussion impacted her ability to continue in sales, she switched gears to keep a promise to a dying friend to write a book.

That book is now a series. The first two—*Friend Grief and Anger: When Your Friend Dies and No One Gives A Damn* and *Friend Grief and AIDS: Thirty Years of Burying Our Friends*—were published in Spring, 2013. Future books in the series (scheduled for the fall of 2013 and winter, 2014) will address grieving a friend in the military and workplace grief.

Her freelance articles have appeared on grief and writing blogs as well as *Windy City Times* and the *Chicago Tribune*. In addition, she feeds her reading habit by reviewing a wide variety of books on BroadwayWorld.com. A native St. Louisan, she's a lifelong Cardinals fan and will gladly take on any comers in musical theatre trivia. Her website, www.FriendGrief.com, was named one of the top ten grief support websites in 2012.

www.ingramcontent.com/pod-product-compliance
Lightning Source LLC
Chambersburg PA
CBHW072018290426
44109CB00018B/2281